Jesus and Buddha: A (

(A comparative study on the teachings of Jesus

and Buddha)

By

Sonny Shanks

"In the world there is sorrow. I can give you rest." - Jesus

"Life is full of suffering. I teach on its cause and cessation." - Buddha

Intro

I am a lifetime Christian. For forty years I was a Protestant Evangelical. I have studied the Bible, taught the Bible, wrote books on the Bible, and have received formal degrees in biblical studies from multiple colleges. All this Bible knowledge eventually led me to the truth of Eucharist being the actual 'body and blood' of Jesus, and as a result brought me home to the Catholic Church. I converted in 2012.

At the same time however, I have always had an affinity for Asian culture and philosophy. This included anything from their cooking (with its emphasis on healthy foods), to gardening techniques, to outdoor decking and landscaping, to what seemed to be in their settings an ever-present nearness of running water (as in a brook or stream). The focus of all this seemed to me to be on life and living.

I studied martial arts for several years too and was struck by their emphasis on *peace*. Besides the exercise components, I was also introduced there to the idea of 'yin yang.' This was explained to me in very basic terms that 'for every action there is a reaction.' I would later come to a fuller understanding of yin yang as pertaining to the Asian concept of *Dualism*: two equal opposites working in tandem. As opposed to 'good vs. bad,' an Asian studies professor once told me to think about dualism the same way we think about breathing. "There is an inhale and an exhale" she said. "Opposites but equal, and both are required. All of creation works like this." As part of all this I found I was continually encountering words such as harmony, tranquility, and serenity.

Somewhere along the way I was also introduced to the idea of *karma*. This too was explained to me in very basic terms and said to be something along the lines of 'what goes around comes around,' 'the good you do comes back to you,' and 'life has a way of evening things out.' There was again this idea of balance.

I never found any of this to be in conflict with my Christian faith. In fact, as *teaching tenets* it all seemed consistent *with* my faith. Any of the Asians I'd ever met or known (through work, school, travel or even my own neighborhood) had always seemed to be soft spoken, humble, and well-mannered people of peace. They seemed to be plugged into something and were living it out on a daily basis. As far as my circle of acquaintances, I knew of no Asians who'd been involved in money, power, or sex scandals. They all seemed happy with their state of affairs and content to just mind their own business.

On the other hand, I was forced to admit that many of my fellow Christians had not always been glowing examples of the faith. Besides scandals, in-fighting and squabbling seemed to be the norm. This was not only between denominations, but locally in-house, at the regular weekly Sunday service. I'd seen and heard of so many church-splits that I began to hear of a new term being used in Christian-speak: *'un-churched.'* This meant Christians who didn't go to church anymore because they'd just been too turned off by it all. Some had moved to generic non-denominational experiences that 'had Jesus in there somewhere,' others were studying at home, and others had simply 'dialed it back' to being Christian *in name only*. More than one person over the years had told me "I'm giving up on church!"

While working through all this and continuing on as a Christian, I nonetheless began to study Asian religions in earnest. Although there were a wide variety of them, most found their origins with a person they called 'the Buddha.' Believed by many to have been Chinese, Buddha was actually from India and was Hindu. Buddha had found Hinduism to be a faith based on *rejection* and *denial* of this world. It mandated a solitary life of poverty, meditative trances, and various starvation techniques, all of which were designed to help one refute or otherwise escape this world. There ought to be a way Buddha thought, to be spiritual while actually *living in this world* and embracing/celebrating the life herein. His solution was the so-called 'Middle Path.'[1] This path was about going through daily life and living as a spiritual exercise unto itself. In other words, *living in this world* became a religious practice, done on the daily, and *outside* of temples.

I found this to be extremely refreshing, and despite what I'd heard so often in church, completely consistent with the words of Jesus. Jesus never said we were to be against all things, avoid people, deny this life in general, or that we should be in a hurry to escape it. He never said we should all try to get to Heaven as quickly as possible and ignore our lives in the here-and-now in the meantime. As a Jew, Jesus would have loved life and embraced God's creation. Many of his teachings concerned 'the Kingdom,' and it is plain from context he was talking about this present world of ours. As part of this, Jesus taught that all people were equal in God's sight and should live in harmony with each other and nature. This equilibrium gets upset he said, when people's selfish desires are allowed to take over and go unchecked. This sounded an awful lot like

---

[1] The word Buddhism itself is said to mean 'a middle way.'

Buddha saying that people foolishly spend their lives trying to accrue wealth and possessions, and believing this to be happiness. This in turn sounded an awful lot like Jesus saying that "You cannot love both God and money" (Matt. 6:24).

As I studied on I kept encountering similarities in the teachings. In readings and lectures at school I was introduced to another new term, 'the Christian Buddhist.' These were Christians who were keeping Jesus as the center of their faith, but were open and welcoming to a lot of what Buddha had to say too. This made sense to me. None of what I was encountering in Buddhism was particularly new (as far as daily living tenets), but it was being said in a *new way*. I could see there being such a thing as a Christian Buddhist.

To be sure, there were differences concerning the soul, the afterlife, and the nature of any kind of supernatural realm. There were differences concerning this supernatural realm's impact and intersection with/on our present realm: blessings, miracles, gifts, powers, and the existence of saints, angels, and demons. As part of this there were differences in prayers, rituals and practices. There were huge differences concerning so-called 'end times,' especially since Buddhism doesn't have any kind of primary Devil character. There's also no special emphasis in Buddhism on 'Buddha's mother.'

However, in a majority of teachings about the how-to's of our worldly lives, Jesus and Buddha often seemed to be saying *exactly* the same thing. In this book I will examine these similarities. I will begin first though, with a brief look at the two historical figures of Jesus and Buddha.[2]

---

[2] Note to reader: since most Christian readers will likely have a Bible and are used to seeing scripture references given at the end of the sentence where used, in most cases I will do that here too. As most of my Biblical points are straight exposition I have not relied on external sources. I have used multiple translations and in some cases lift the verse directly, and in others use a paraphrase of several to deliver a clearer, more readable thought. Since my Buddhism points may require additional explanation, I have sourced them and put them in footnotes along the bottom and at book's end. This will hopefully make for an easier read yet have the references readily available should the reader wish further information.

1 - The Real Jesus

Many in today's pop culture place Jesus somewhere on a line that has Santa Claus on one end and a surfer dude on the other. In modern art and media he has been westernized to the point of looking like a businessman, politician, or Hollywood actor. In these depictions he appears to be from the mid-west area of the U.S. Many folks believe Jesus was an American.

In reality, the historical Jesus was born into a *Jewish family* in *Palestine* some 2000 years ago. The word 'Christ' is not a last name but an honorific that means 'Messiah.' According to scripture he was the son of Joseph and Mary. As such he would have initially been simply known as 'Jesus son of Joseph.' Later as the family spent time in the areas of Galilee and Nazareth, Jesus would have also been called 'Jesus of Galilee' or 'Jesus of Nazareth.'

Scripture says Jesus had a miraculous birth. There were dreams and visions involved (from both Joseph and Mary), a 'virgin birth,' the 'star of Bethlehem,' a heralding of the birth by 'the Heavenly hosts,' and 'the Three Wise Men.'

At some point post-birth, life settled down for Jesus, Mary, and Joseph and they transitioned into being a typical Jewish working-class family. Scripture says Joseph was a carpenter. Many historians believe Joseph was significantly older than Mary, was a widower, and already had adult children from that previous marriage and with whom he ran his carpentry business.

The only other information the Bible gives of Jesus' early years is the so-called 'temple incident' of (Lk. 2:42-47). Here a twelve-year old Jesus gets separated from his family and is later found in the synagogue. He is in the company of the scholars and is said to have been astounding them with his questions and answers. After this the Bible simply says that Jesus returned home with his parents, was 'obedient to them in all things', gained 'wisdom and stature,' and 'grew in favor with God and man' (Lk. 2:51-52).

Scripture immediately 'skips ahead' to Jesus at 30. This leaves a gap of some eighteen years, commonly referred to as 'the lost years.' These missing years represent over half of Jesus' life. Speculation abounds as to what he did and where he went during this period. He may have traveled abroad and studied, or he may have simply stayed home and worked in his dad's carpentry shop. One possible clue is found in Matt. 13:55-56, where it shows that Jesus was recognized and known by others in his home area. This would likely not have been the case if he had just returned from being abroad for nearly twenty years.

In any case, at or around age 30 Jesus began a short ministry that would only last three and a half years. It was a ministry of miracles, signs, and wonders. It climaxed with his arrest, trial, crucifixion, resurrection, and ascension. Laying aside the supernatural aspects of all of this (which are matters of faith), what Jesus left behind was a significant body of teachings. Most of these were based around ideas like self-denial, self-control, self-sacrifice, and putting others first.[3]

After his departure Jesus' message would be circulated far and wide. This included it reaching the West, where it seemed to flourish and grow, even more so than in Jerusalem.

This is the actual historic Jesus. Any kind of Santa or surfer Jesus, or business/politics/mid-west Jesus, is an add-on based on misunderstanding and/or cultural convenience.

---

[3] Some of the dates and various details of Jesus' story are not universally agreed to, but these are the highlights.

2 - The Real Buddha

Many in today's pop culture place Buddha somewhere on a line that has 'Maitreya' on one end and Confucius on the other. Maitreya is the fat and bald and jolly character folks might see on display at a typical Asian restaurant. He represents success, wealth, joviality, and happiness. As such he could also be seen as a Santa Claus type persona. Although primarily a *future* figure his blessings of plenty may still be sought in the present. Confucius on the other hand, was an actual person from ancient China. He was a philosopher, politician, and overall wise man. He is usually associated in the West with logic, reasoning, and catch phrases such as "Confucius say so-and-so…." Either way in modern art Buddha is usually depicted as Asian. Many folks believe Buddha was Chinese.

In reality the historic Buddha was born into a *Hindu family* in *India* some 2500 years ago. His name was Siddhartha Shakyamuni. 'Buddha' is an honorific that would come later and means 'Enlightened One.' Unlike Jesus, he was born into a family of wealth and power: a family that was part of the ruling class. In fact, he spent all his youth sheltered away inside a castle. Early on certain holy men predicted he would become a significant figure in either politics or religion, or both. Siddhartha received a quality education, became a practicing Hindu, and eventually married and had kids. As with Jesus, his next significant life event would happen at around age 30.

At this time Siddhartha decided to venture outside the castle walls for the first time. Once out and among the people he encountered what are known as 'the four passing sights.' These included a sick man, an old man, a dead man, and a monk-type/religious seeker. He had never seen any of these before, and the culture shock sent him on a years-long journey to learn what it all meant and how he should respond.

Raised Hindu, he first went to the Hindu masters. Each one he studied under emphasized a different meditative trance or starvation technique. All of them lived in poverty. As mentioned above, the idea was that our present world was evil, and that man wasn't supposed to be here. Starvation and trances were designed to take a person to 'another place.' The belief was that this other place was somehow more real, better, and was where man actually belonged.

While Siddhartha agreed that there was evil *in* the world, he disagreed that the *world itself* was evil. Regularly starving or trancing oneself to escape it would be pointless. If the plight of man is that he is born in the beginning, dies at the end, and suffers in between, and the *world* isn't the reason, then there must be some other cause. Similar to Jesus' 'missing years,' Siddhartha separated himself from his masters and went into exile to find this cause. He vowed to not come back until he'd learned of it, mastered it, and had solutions to it. Some believe this exile lasted five years.

At some point he sat under a fiscus or so-called 'Bodhi' tree and touched or slapped the ground, calling in the Earth as a witness and help to his quest. Some type of supernatural epiphany happened next. Siddhartha saw/visited the next/higher realm, battled demonic forces, and was ministered to by benevolent celestials, all of which gave him their allegiance. When the smoke cleared Siddhartha stood alone and had become the 'Enlightened One' or 'the Buddha.' The answers he'd been seeking had all now been revealed. He also found that he now had supernatural abilities. These included telepathy, healing, levitation, teleportation, and more.[4] He returned to his former

---

[4] For comparison see especially Jesus' 'walking through a wall' or 'floating away into the sky,' John 20:26 and Acts 1:9 respectively.

masters, shared his story, his new insights, and demonstrated his new abilities. They became his first students.[5]

Again and as above, laying aside the supernatural aspects of all this, what remain are the teachings. Chief among these is the core tenet that although life is full of suffering, suffering itself is not an automatic given, and doesn't have to be so. Suffering has a cause, and through his enlightenment experience Buddha had learned that this cause is 'change.' People don't like it, don't want it, aren't prepared for it, don't react well to it, and have a tough time getting past it. For many people change often infers some kind of loss. This may be something tangible like property or intangible like a relationship. It can involve health, home, family, job, community, or some other. It may involve a single change or multiple changes, all at the same time. Since life is full of change and change makes people unhappy, Buddha said most people are going to be unhappy most the time. The key to easing this unhappiness or 'suffering' would be in trying to do something about change, or at least people's attitude about change. Buddha would go on to proscribe ways in which people can avoid many unnecessary, negative

---

[5] Some of the dates and various details of Buddha's story are not universally agreed to, but these are the highlights. "The Biography of Buddha." Biographiesonline.net.

changes (often caused by their own actions), and promote instead certain other changes that are of a positive, helpful nature. Most of both of these were based around ideas like self-denial, self-control, self-sacrifice, and putting others first.

Unlike Jesus, Buddha would live on to about age 80 and have plenty of time to travel far and wide and circulate his message. This included it being eventually exported to China and all of Asia, where it seemed to flourish and grow, even more so than in India.

This is the actual historic Buddha. Any kind of Maitreya or Confucius Buddha, or business/politics/Chinese Buddha, is an add-on based on misunderstanding and/or cultural convenience.

3 - The Soul and Sin and the Three Marks of Existence

Both Jesus and Buddha agreed that all people have a nature, essence, or core that allows them to live beyond the grave, *in some kind of form*. Jesus would say that this is because each person has a soul. That soul is made of spiritual stuff and is eternal. A person is born, lives, and dies, and then their soul goes to either Heaven or Hell for all eternity. Within some segments of Christianity there is also the idea of a 'pre-existence' of the soul. This teaches that a person's soul was already in existence in Heaven, prior to their birth. It was there for some undisclosed period, possibly since Creation, and then initially enters this world for the first time when a person is born (or conceived). While it is unclear whether Jesus accepted this idea, either way (pre-existence or creation at conception) a soul would only be 'stopping in' on our world for seventy-something years. It would then go on/back to the next realm and eternity. Jesus would say then, that a soul spends most of its time in the *next* world.

Buddha would say that if a person has a soul it is largely unknown and unknowable. It would be of and about something outside our range of perception and experience, since everything we know and *all we can know* comes from our physical senses of our physical world. This was less against the idea of any kind of soul or spiritual center as it was, post his enlightenment, a reaction to the Hindu belief that given the next world or ours, the next world is the more real of the two.[6] For Buddha our present world of the here-and-now was the more real of the two and the only thing by which we can and ought to live our lives. And the chief concern among all this was the element of change.

Buddha said that if humans continue beyond this life, it is only in the same way that all other animal and plant life continue. A person's essential elements, including any soul, are recycled back into nature and life in general. This is true of any other living thing, whether a dead animal or next year's grass. This is one of the reasons Buddhists do not bury their dead but cremate, to better allow for this recycling.[7] Any spiritual aspects there may

---

[6] Hindus refer to this present world as 'Maya,' or illusion.
[7] This is not a universal hard and fast rule for Buddhists but is true in general and overall. At the same time this also goes against the idea of an eventual end-times 'resurrection,' as is common to almost all strains of Christianity. Here, when a particular body is gone it is simply gone. As there is no expectation that it comes back or is one day 'raised' there is no need to

be to the person are part of this process. Any particular person at any particular time is then necessarily a composite of previous source material, which again would include any soul matter. There is a final resting place and cessation to all this, a cosmic/heavenly realm called 'Nirvana,' but it takes lifetimes to get there and only via enlightenment. Some people will *never* see it: their essentials will just keep cycling and recycling back to this present world indefinitely. Far from a seventy-year stopover then, Buddha would say that souls, such as they are, spend most of their time in *our* world.

Despite this basic disagreement as to the nature of the soul Jesus and Buddha would come back into agreement that deeds done while in the body, *while in our present world*, affect a person both in this life *and* the next. Positive, helpful, beneficial acts yield corresponding results. They *can* also lead to a final resting place in the next. Negative, hurtful, harmful acts yield negative, hurtful, harmful results. They can also prevent/hinder/retard attaining to a final resting place.

---

preserve or otherwise save it. "Buddhists and Funerals." Buddhismwordpress.com.

Jesus would call these negative acts 'sin,' and say that the sufferings that results from them are 'the wages of sin.'[8] He might add that a 'bad tree' produces 'bad fruit,' i.e. bad actions produce bad results. These negative, hurtful deeds could be anything from lust to greed to anger to jealousy to deceit, and the like. Jesus *especially* spoke about the sins of religious hypocrisy and ignoring the poor. If uncorrected, the ultimate end of these unhappy lifestyles is Hell (Matt. 25:29-30, 46).

Buddha condensed much of the above into one of his signature works: 'the Three Marks of Existence.'[9] Here he repeated that life is full of change and change (or fear of change) causes suffering. This is especially true if people try to gain control of life and prevent change by attaching to assumed fixed points, like a presumed spiritual realm. This last Buddha called 'anatman,' which essentially means 'no soul,' or even 'no self.'[10] This again was not a denial of either the soul or of an individual's identity in the real

---

[8] To be sure this exact quote comes from Paul in Rom. 6:23. The point remains the same.

[9] These have been translated a variety of ways but are usually stated as, 1) life is full of suffering, 2) nothing in life is fixed or permanent (impermanence), and 3) this includes the soul. The rendering I prefer is, 1) nothing in life is *unaffected,* 2) including a person's soul, 3) assuming they *are* leads one down useless paths of suffering. "the Three Marks of Existence." Buddhist.org.

[10] For persons in the West a better way to think of 'no soul' might be in thinking in terms of 'no *unaffected* soul.'

world. It was simply Buddha's assertation that attempting to live one's life by abstraction is misguided. Attempting to be alternately led/accused by something that doesn't exist in real space and time is not only unprofitable, it is unwise. It only leads to stress, anxiety, and depression. This necessarily centers Buddhism's focus then, on the present. It establishes that people are better off dealing with the 'what-is' than the 'what-is-not.' And part of the reality of *our* world is that *nothing* is fixed: everything is in a constant process of change. As a part of this process Buddha would naturally say that 'actions matter.' What we do in life, especially vis-à-vis each other, matters. There are actions, results, and consequences. 'No-self' carries the double meaning of acting un-self-ish-ly. These are the keys to good results, good karma, and enlightenment. Without these suffering will continue, and people will just keep coming back (in successive lives) to do more of the same. Buddha's idea of the 'no-self' is then actually quite close to what Jesus might say about 'loving thy neighbor' and 'doing unto others.'

As far as the soul and once around in this life vs. cycling back, the Christian notion of 'Purgatory' provides a possible meeting point between Jesus and Buddha. Purgatory is thought to be a place 'between Heaven and Hell' where imperfect souls go to learn and/or be 'purified.' In this place, which is thought to be a slightly out-of-step existence *with* and not quite *in* our world, souls go to witness the consequences their various misdeeds had on others. There is suffering on the part of the soul and in some cases 'burning' (which may or may not be literal). At some point and after a time, the soul processes on to Heaven. Purgatory is accepted by certain segments of Christianity and not by others. It is unclear whether Jesus accepted the idea, but adherents point to his 'Rich man and Lazarus' parable of Luke 16:19-31 as a possible endorsement. In the story a rich man is in or on some kind of spiritual place/plane and is witnessing family and friends back on Earth. They are making the same mistakes he made and are suffering for it. He is suffering for his own misdeeds and suffering while watching theirs. He knows that unless they change their ways they are headed for the same place as him.

Purgatory suggests then a very Buddhist-like notion that some souls stay in this realm and do not immediately move on to a *final*, eternal place. Even if only as an observer and not specifically in a body, the soul is nonetheless in our realm and suffering/learning. It must complete this process before moving on. Presumably if it resists or refuses this learning or 'enlightenment' it would just stay in Purgatory, or in other words *here*. If Jesus did accept *this* notion, then he and Buddha would have been closer on the idea of suffering souls than might initially be apparent.

In some strains of Christianity, especially Catholicism, there is even the idea that the living may pray for souls in Purgatory, that their trials/purifications may be completed, and that they may move on to Heaven. Buddhism has these practices too, believing they are 'guiding' in nature, and most effective if done within three weeks of the person's passing.[11]

Jesus and Buddha do find common ground then on sin, suffering, and the soul. Buddha said suffering is a mark of human existence. Jesus said people should expect *troubles* today and *worries* tomorrow (Matt. 6:34). Both agree that choices and actions done now, reverberate now, in the future, and beyond the grave.

---

[11] The 'lag time' between a soul leaving a body and going on to the next realm or the next person is debatable in either faiths. As to Christianity, one might scripturally argue in favor of instantaneous soul migration. Traditionally though, there has been a longstanding belief in the 'three-day rule' i.e. that it takes a soul three days to get to its destination. This is likely rooted in the idea of Jesus spending 'three days in the tomb.' As to Buddhism, as mentioned above, the idea is that the migration may take three weeks (or longer). An assisting prayer goes like this: "May all beings be filled with loving kindness, May all beings be well, May all beings be peaceful and at ease, May all beings be happy and free from suffering." "Buddhists and Funerals." Ibid.

4 - Self-Control and Attachment

Self-control, or the lack thereof, is a central theme in most religions. Jesus and Buddha taught on it too. The issue of a self-centered 'all about me' culture was as big a problem in their day as it is today. Much of this involves money, as people then and now believe(d) money *can* buy them happiness.

Jesus famously said however, that 'You cannot love (or serve) both God and money" (Matt. 6:24). He advised a certain 'rich young ruler' to "Sell all you have and give to the poor, and then you will have treasure in Heaven" (Lk. 18:22). He told the story of a man who had so much wealth he couldn't contain it all. The man said to himself "I'm going to have to tear down my old barns and build new ones, so I'll have more room for it all!" Jesus said however that the man died that very night. All his wealth went to somebody else and Jesus referred to him as a 'fool.' (Lk. 12:16-20). His money and possessions all led to naught; it neither saved him in this life nor the next. In the story already mentioned above, a certain other 'rich man' died and went to Purgatory/Hell: during his lifetime he had ignored the poor, even when they were on his doorstep (Lk. 16:19-31).

To people obsessed with money and possessions Jesus posed the question, "What do you benefit if you gain the whole world but lose your soul?" (Mk. 8:36). He told certain others (who had asked him how they should live) that they ought to "Do your job, be fair, don't make false accusations, and be content with your pay" (Lk. 3:12-14). In general Jesus summed up his ideas on happiness and self-fulfillment through money by saying "Seek ye *first* the kingdom of God" (Matt. 6:33-34). This necessarily implies a need to not be caught up in the things or 'cares of this world.' Just following the crowd is 'detestable to God,' said Jesus (Lk. 16:15). He taught that the proper use of excess money is to "benefit others and make friends for yourself." This will help a person get to Heaven (Lk. 16:19). All of this involves self-control.

Buddha would say that all of the above is an issue with 'attachment.' Attachment is again, an attempt to stop or block *change*. People form attachments to things, and exert control/ownership of them, so as to get their way. If they can get their way they want to keep on getting it. Many people again, especially in today's consumer world, think this is attainable via money but in the center of it all really is relationships. Sometimes it's about advancing of one's position in life, other times it involves no more than the regular ups and downs *of* life, but always vis-à-vis other people. It is about a desired power to gain control and to stop change, or at least call the shots on change. Buddha said all such hopes and expectations only lead ultimately to suffering, because 'nothing is in our control.'

His solution was in 'non-attachments.' This is sometimes misinterpreted by the West to mean that Buddha was advocating 'don't care about anything and you won't be hurt if/when it goes away.' Rather Buddha was saying that imagined control is only an illusion. A lifetime of such pursuits may yield the illusion of control, but in reality nothing is fixed or permanent and everything changes just the same. A life like this is due to a *fear* of change. All of life's problems, Buddha felt, were/are caused by people acting on their fears and by living self-centeredly and via attachments. All of this kind of action, reaction, and karma leads to suffering. *Fear* of change leads to suffering. *Actual* change leads to more suffering. Change is the issue. Attachment is the problem. Non-attachment is the solution.

Buddha held that perhaps the greatest thing to which people attach is *themselves*. All of this pursuit of money and power and position is an attempt to realize and hold onto an idealized version of self. It is all ultimately self-defeating though, as no one ever gets all their hopes and dreams, needs and wants, fulfilled and *that* endlessly. No one gets to get their way, keep on getting their way (to the exclusion and even expense of others), and never experience loss or at least change. And the conundrum is, that even if they did, they still wouldn't be happy. There would only be disappointment along the lines of 'Is that all there is? Is there no more?' What would follow could only be listlessness and boredom, futility and fragility.[12] An attachment to self then leads only to a state of continual suffering. Buddha would say the ultimate non-attachment lies in denying the self, denying the self *itself*, and moving forward *without* a self or better yet with a 'no-self.' Jesus would come remarkably close to this with his comments on self-control, to the point of there being a *denial* of self, to the point of it being as if there *was* no self. This leads naturally into a discussion of both's ideas of the 'self.'

---

[12] The Greek Epicureans believed that unlimited time and unlimited resources would eventually lead only to 'diminishing returns.' At some point, a person's satisfaction with a thing or situation tops out and further frequency yields decreasing satisfaction and/or contentment.

5 - The 'Old Man' vs. the 'No-Self'

For centuries a person was identified by their place among several subsets of sets. Firstly, a person was a 'human.' They then might be said to be male or female. They might be of a certain nationality. They might be young or old. They might be a brother or a sister. They might be married or single. They might be both child and parent. They could be a grandparent. They would think of themselves as being, and be thought of as being, part of a family line and having a 'family tree.' All of these various subsets would help a person to identify themselves and find and mark their place in life.[13]

Along with this, and also for centuries prior, people identified and placed themselves, and were known by others, by what they did in life. This might be a vocation: farmer, soldier, poet, preacher, teacher, student, butcher, baker, candlestick maker.

---

[13] This way of thinking was formalized, at least for the West, by Aristotle's famous work *Categories and Topics*.

Beyond vocation though, there was very much the idea of being identified by your actions. Character traits especially, were seen as being equated with a person's actions. 'So-and-so is brave,' 'so-and-so is kind,' or even 'so-and-so is always on time.' Taken together these gave *real* ways to find and identify oneself amongst one's peers and in life in general.

Circa 1500 C. E. (A. D.) the so-called 'Enlightenment Era' began, first in Europe, and would continue on for about 300 years, with eventual worldwide influence. The importance of this period cannot be overstated, as Philosophers/thinkers sought to rethink the idea of 'self.' The traditional tether points were replaced by abstraction. A person now identified and measured themselves against a hypothetical construct. This hypothetical construct was called 'the self.' It had no existence in real time or space, no connection to family, or vocation, or actual deeds. Some refer to this construct as 'the Ought,' as in 'ought to be.' An alternate self, identity and realm was imagined, which was ideal, and persons began to compare themselves to this. It might also be thought of as a movement to a culture of 'the One.' This became a basis for, and major driver behind, a changing social, political, and especially *economic* system where the idea was for people to identify themselves and find their position in life by measuring against *their own* imagined ideal. *Naturally* everyone felt they were *naturally* 'entitled to it all.' All traditional relationships became replaced with and by a single new one: *a state of war*.[14] Cash and currency, as opposed to land holdings, cattle, etc., became the way to measure prosperity, i.e. 'purchase power,' and this type of monetary system became available and easily distributable to all. The idea of actually being able to attain 'the good life,' with its pertinent definitions, became the new social/societal norm. It was the thing all people were going by and working towards, and the means by which they identified themselves *and* related to others, though as an abstract concept not existing in real fact or substance. Society moved nonetheless towards a culture of 'self-centeredness,' as the approved and accepted and commonly understood norm.[15]

---

[14] 16th/17th Century English philosopher Thomas Hobbes did arguably the most work on this idea in his signature piece *the Leviathan*. He argued that the only way to have 'peace on Earth' was to have a government mandated and controlled free enterprise system where everyone is allowed, even encouraged, to seek and pursue and realize their full potential, equally, to the exclusion of all else. This became the sole identifier of self. All else he viewed as 'unknown.' Those that refused to participate were to be put in prison, exiled, or executed. He actually tried to underwrite and authorize this model with scripture! Most of the modern world embraces Hobbes' consumerism ideas as it has become nearly impossible to function, individually or as a nation, outside of them.

[15] In her well-known essay "What is Freedom?" writer Hannah Arendt said this mindset has become so ingrained in modernity that nothing short of a global cataclysm - where people are not able to buy or sell due to the demise of the physical infrastructures of consumerism - will ever bring change.

Measuring against such an imagined realm, which contains only perfection and never any downsides, not only cuts all relationship ties, replacing them with 'competition from the enemy,' it leaves most people most of the time short and wanting. Despite what might seem to be the apparent and obvious problems of such a scheme, this model has remained in place up to the present. Self as a manifestation of an imagined 'Ought' is the only relationship that counts: the relationship of *self to self*. People have a relationship with themselves, or perhaps with the money that enables and empowers them to realize self.

Jesus and Buddha have clear and concise things to say on this subject. Besides above citations such as "You cannot love God and money" and "What does it profit a man to gain the whole world and yet lose his soul," Jesus spoke much about "Taking up your cross."[16] This is an idea that is opposite of self-service; it is all about serving others, even when it hurts. He also famously advised to 'consider the lilies' of the field, and how even the richest person with the finest wardrobe (and make-up and cosmetic surgeries) cannot approach them in beauty. And the lilies labored and slaved

---

[16] Matt. 16:24.

and worried about their appearance and station not. Jesus was essentially saying 'be like that.'[17]

Jesus taught his followers that all people are born with a selfish tendency or 'sin nature.' James, the 'brother of the Lord,' said this about it: "What causes conflicts and quarrels among you (all people)? Don't they come from the passions at war within you? You crave what you do not have. You kill and covet but are unable to obtain. You quarrel and fight. You do not have, because you do not ask. And when you do ask, you do not receive, because you ask with wrong motives, that you may squander it on your pleasures" (James 4:2)[18] Jesus said nothing could stop these tendencies short of a full-fledged conversion experience, to the point of 'starting over' or being 'born again' (John 3:3). The solution of a new birth experience sets up a dichotomy between the former and current version of a person. In Christianity, this former version is called 'the old man,' the new version is called 'the new

---

[17] Luke 12:27.

[18] In Catholicism James is thought to be the brother of the Lord in that he was a child of Joseph by a previous and deceased wife, with whom Joseph may have had five or more additional children too. Some Bible translations have 'brother' as 'cousin' or generic for relative. In the Protestant world it is assumed Jesus was the first of Joseph and Mary's children, and that they went on to have others. In the former Jesus would have had several older step-brothers and sisters. In the latter he would have had several younger half-brothers and sisters. Matt. 13:55-56.

man.' Although the whole time it's exactly the same person, the converted person is to act like the old man no longer exists. This takes practice.[19]

The new man is to deny the wants of the old man; to deny the wants of the self. This has the effect of weakening the old man to the point of starvation. Once so weakened the old man no longer exerts influence on the new person's life. Paul says to "do nothing out of selfish ambition, and don't try to impress others" (Phi 2:3).[20] This alone might cover most people's issues. He takes it further though and says to "be crucified with Christ," so that the old man is essentially *killed off* (Gal. 2:20). He says to not "copy the behaviors and customs of this world" but to be "dead to sin" and "transformed" (Rom. 6:11, 12:2). Paul says the central thing in life, "the only thing that counts," is this transformation (Gal. 6:15).[21]

---

[19] To the idea that faith must be an ongoing project James would famously say: "Faith without works is dead" (Ja. 2:26).

[20] Paul was not one of the original twelve Apostles but would later meet the risen Lord while on a road trip to the city of Damascus (Acts 9:4). Besides this initial encounter, scholars believe Paul was taken *somewhere* by Jesus and trained for *some time* before starting his own ministry. Although opinions vary as to the location of the training - anything from Europe to *Heaven* - most agree on a time frame of three years.

[21] Jude would later 'one-up' James' 'faith without works is dead' comment by saying that such people are no better than irrational animals or 'beasts,' and are "*twice* dead" (Jude 10-12).

Buddha's contribution to the conversation is straightforward and has flawless logic: selfish pursuits are pointless because there is no self to please. There is no self to which one might affix, attach, go by, be led by, or by which to be judged, criticized or condemned.[22] If a person is alive and in this world it's because of reincarnation, meaning the person has been here at least one time previously, likely more. As such, no person alive on Earth at any particular time can be a fixed, unchanged, unique, one-of-a-kind self.[23]

In teachings called 'Skandhas,' Buddha shows that people are a combination of senses, surroundings, desires, and mental conditions *and* conditioning. The drive to satisfy self is part of this conditioning. As there is no self, only temporary things and temporary situations, being led by self is misguided error. Thinking that one can feed impermanence with more impermanence and get permanence is fallacy and illusion. Said another way,

---

[22] Post-Enlightenment philosopher Immanuel Kant would suggest something similar in saying that there is no theoretical realm of the 'Ought,' and that if there is it cannot be known by humans, as all we have to go by are our thoughts and words, all of which are formed by our real senses of the real physical world.

[23] Where 'reincarnation' appears here it is for convenience only. Strictly speaking, a Buddhist might say they do not believe in reincarnation as reincarnation implies a person has a 'self' to come back or be reincarnated, which they would say a person does not. A Buddhist priest friend once told me "We don't believe in reincarnation. We believe in a continuation of life but with change."

the drive to live selfishly and attempt to build something permanent and lasting is useless: there is no self to satisfy and nothing is permanent and lasting. Permanence is what a person seeks so as to establish fixed points in life. Fixed points allow a person to move within a system and seek control. Control prevents change, or at least allows for some *control of change,* and that to a person's liking.

Since there is no self, nothing permanent, and no stopping change, the key to a happy life in Buddhism is to accept change, live unselfishly, and not worry about the rest (especially since you can't control it). Anything beyond the basic necessities of this life are unnecessary.[24] Anything beyond this produces suffering, not the least of which is more reincarnation cycles where a person just keeps coming back for more of the same; more suffering in pursuit of pleasing an imagined self. A person must see past the changing physical and impermanent world, and into the unchanging, non-physical, permanent world. This yields Enlightenment. As with Christianity, Buddhism sets up a dichotomy: old vs. new rephrased as self vs. no-self. Although here

---

[24] The Epicureans agreed here too, saying that any pleasures beyond the removal of pain were unneeded and unnecessary. If anything, they only cause disruptions and 'disturbances' in life. Many believe the Epicureans knew of and were influenced by Buddhism, since in Buddha's day and afterwards trade routes were beginning to open up between East and West.

again and the whole time it's exactly the same person, the converted person is to deny the previous version to the point of it not existing. This takes practice.[25]

Jesus and Buddha would both then deliver stinging rebuttals to the modern self-driven consumer lifestyle. They would both see error in pursuing a life of and according to the old man/self. It would be a lifestyle of sin and attachments, and one that only causes suffering. It would not yield happiness or control. It does not prevent change.

Both would recommend a changed attitude and mindset; one that practices at denying the old man and in being so selfless that it is as if there is *no self*. This involves faith, works, deeds, results. In a world of the real, this would go to re-establish traditional tether points of identity through connections *and* actions, especially vis-s-vis one's fellow human beings.

---

[25] One such practice common and traditional to both Christianity and Buddhism is fasting. It is practicing at denying the wants of the body, the old man, the self. This is viewed as a visible, tangible way to practice self-control.

6 - The Golden Rule and the Silver Rule

Jesus said he had not come "to abolish the Law but to fulfill it" (Matt. 5:17). He said not one "jot or tittle" of the law could be ignored if a person wanted to be happy in *this* life and make it to Heaven in the *next* (Lk. 16:17). 'The Law' was seen was handed down to the people from Moses (around 1300 B.C.E.) and written by God himself (Ex. 31:18). While much of this has come down to us today as a list of 'Thou shalt nots,' it actually originates with the OT's Ten Commandments:

1) Thou shalt not have any other gods before me.
2) Thou shalt not make unto thee any graven image, nor bow down to it, nor serve it.
3) Thou shalt not take the Lord's name in vain.
4) Thou shalt not work on the Sabbath.
5) Thou shalt not dishonor thy father or thy mother.
6) Thou shalt not commit murder.
7) Thou shalt not commit adultery.
8) Thou shalt not steal.
9) Thou shalt not give false witness (lie) about others.

10) Thou shalt not covet thy neighbor's things.[26]

In Matt. 7:12 Jesus would later distill all this down into what is commonly called 'the Golden Rule':

"Do unto others as you would have them do unto you."

Buddhism has its 'Thou shalt nots' as well.[27] They are called 'the Five Precepts' and are:

1) Do not lie.

2) Do not steal.

3) Do not murder.

4) Do not have extra-marital affairs.

5) Do not use alcohol excessively.[28]

Buddha would similarly condense these into a central thought, the so-called 'Silver Rule':

"Do not do to others anything that you would not want others to do to you."

---

[26] The Ten Commandments can be found in several places in the Bible, but first appear in their entirety in Exodus 20:2-17.
[27] Whereas Buddhism predates Christianity by some five hundred years, in this case the nod goes to Judaism, which would predate Buddhism by approximately the same.
[28] The use of 'thou' and 'thee' is unique to Europe and the West. With an Eastern orientation the Five Precepts simply say 'do not.'

Some have argued that this is a strategy of simply 'do no harm.' As such it based more on ideas like cause and effect, actions and karma, results and consequences, and less on what is arguably a guilt-based system. Either way, and laying aside the disconnects the two faiths have as to a Supreme Deity, and allowing for both simplified reductions, as far as a working game plan for most people's daily lives the two are almost identical. Whether the Golden Rule or the Silver Rule, Jesus and Buddha seem to be saying the same thing.

7 - Salvation and the Four Noble Truths

As mentioned above, in the West there is the idea that each person is unique, a 'one of,' and has a soul. To do or act wrongfully in this life is considered 'sin.' There are repercussions for self and others because of one's sins, and at death the person must answer for them. Unless they somehow are forgiven or 'pardoned,' they are sent to and punished in Hell.

The way out of this is to be 'saved.' While Jesus said all sins can be forgiven and that's God's grace knows no bounds, he at the same time reaffirmed the existence of Hell. There is wide disagreement among the different Christian strains as to how much sin is 'too much,' and as to how exactly one is pardoned or saved, but the basic idea is one of a redemptive, forgiving act that comes from God to the person, once that person has 'repented,' or otherwise seen the error of their ways. This changed attitude, mindset and lifestyle is said to put the person on a new path. It is said to cause a change in the person and re-make them into something/someone new: no longer self-obsessed and pleasure seeking, but meek, humble, and putting others first. They have quit sinning, or are at least trying to do so, have turned over a new leaf, and are changed. They are better off now in this life, and are looking forward to the next, where they will be in Heaven.

In Christianity, all of this is referred to as 'salvation,' and in every strain it is available and made possible by Jesus, through his death on the cross. He essentially and voluntarily took on the penalty for our sins. If we accept this, and again there is a *wide* spectrum on how it is that we do this, then we are said to be 'saved.'

Buddhism has been called a 'thinking person's religion.' There is less an idea of 'sin' than there is 'error.' Due to incorrect thinking people act wrongfully and it leads to unhappiness for them and others. The punishment is immediate and apparent through the negative results and consequences of one's actions. The sin or error was done now, the results happen now. There is not, for the most part, an idea of continuing to punish the person beyond the grave. In fact, in Buddhism the person doesn't even to get to stay in the grave. They keep coming back to this life until they correct their thinking and their choices and their lifestyle.

If Buddha would say acting wrongfully is an unenlightened lifestyle, then to do right comes from being enlightened. 'Enlightenment' is the Buddhist equivalent of salvation, and the path to a better, changed life and lifestyle. A person is saved from themselves and their erroneous way of thinking and acting. If they learn their lesson(s) they don't have to come back to this life again. This is good since, according to Buddha, this life contains only suffering (caused by the unenlightened actions of people).

As part of this 'thinking person's religion,' Buddha laid out 'Four Noble Truths':

1) All of life is full of suffering.
2) Suffering comes from somewhere, it is not an automatic given.
3) If the source can be identified suffering can be eased or ceased.
4) The source has been identified; suffering can be eased or ceased.

The source, though this seems oversimplified and obvious, to the point of being almost humorous, is 'to quit being bad.' This again is flawless logic and against which it is not possible to argue. It again lacks a sin component, and as a result perhaps a guilt component, but leaves the person with the reality of stark truth: negative thoughts, words, and actions yield negative results. It can't possibly get any plainer than that. Many people in the West, somewhat turned off by religion per se, especially in a day of the religious right as a political entity, have been drawn to this non-judgmental yet matter-of-fact nature of Buddhism.

Jesus and Buddha however, though taking different tact's, would again be saying the same essentials: a person's natural, normal tendency is to act in self-interest. This does not deliver benefits but rather does them and others harm. Everyone everywhere acting in this same way sends out wave after wave of bad results, all intersecting with and crashing into each other, and creating new and worse results: results in which the initial person may not have even had a hand. This creates a life full, a world full, of suffering.

Jesus and Buddha would agree that the key and elemental solution is in *change*. Jesus might call it salvation, Buddha might call it enlightenment, but either way the idea is stop current wrongful actions, try something different, make a change, and take a new path.[29]

---

[29] The Four Noble Truths have also been translated a variety of ways. A convenient version can be found here: https://www.thoughtco.com/the-four-noble-truths-450095.

8 - The Beatitudes and the Eightfold Path to Enlightenment

Both Jesus and Buddha laid out ideas on how people ought to live, especially if they want to be happy. For Jesus, much of his teachings on this are found in his so-called 'Beatitudes.'[30] For Buddha, much of his teachings on this are found in his so-called 'Eightfold Path to Enlightenment.'[31]

Jesus said a person would be "blessed" or "happy" (an alternate translation) if they were "poor in spirit." It's interesting that he mentions this beatitude first as 'poor in spirit' is generally thought to mean having the opposite kind of 'spirit' or attitude from those who are materially rich. A poor person doesn't put on airs, isn't consumed with money and possessions, and is usually quite grateful when they get something. They view it as a gift and not as something 'they were owed.' This attitude or mindset fits right in with non-attachment.

---

[30] The Beatitudes can be found in Matt. 5:3-10. Luke 6 has a version too, along with four 'woes.'
[31] A convenient version of the Eightfold Path to Enlightenment can be found here: http://www.buddhanet.net/e-learning/8foldpath.htm.

Jesus says that "Those who mourn will be comforted." In order to mourn, a person must have feelings for others: a person must care about someone or something besides themselves. Jesus says such people "will be comforted." This too suggests that while mourning is normal and natural, at some point there needs to be a 'moving on.' Receiving comfort helps with this. It also suggests that people who don't mourn, people who lack sympathy and empathy, likely care only about themselves. They may think they are happy with their stuff but are likely alone in this world, and when they die they die alone and unmourned.

"Blessed are the meek" is in line with the above: meek people aren't trying to game and control others. They will be happier and have more peace of mind than those who do try to manipulate others. "Hungering and thirsting for righteousness" implies equitable actions and fair play. 'Being merciful' carries with it the reciprocity of receiving mercy in time of need. A 'purity of heart' suggests right thinking, speaking, and acting. Here a person will not have to second-guess themselves and will especially not have to worry about repercussions from telling lies. This again fosters peace and happiness. 'Peacemakers' and other advocates of playing fair, getting along, sharing, and working things out amicably, will all be called 'children of God' according to Jesus.

His final beatitude is worth singling out because, like in his first one, Jesus says people - who suffer because of righteousness - will receive the 'kingdom of Heaven.' Anytime Jesus says the 'kingdom of Heaven' or 'kingdom of God,' he is talking about the qualities and attributes of such a realm being present in our realm now: brought in by our actions now.

Buddha preferences his steps to enlightenment with the word 'rightful.' His first is that a person ought to have 'rightful speech.' Words can help, harm, lift up, or bring down. They can be positive and reinforcing or meaningless and empty. Jesus said as much with: "The bad words that come out of your mouth are what make you unclean" (Matt. 15:11). Words lead to action and Buddha's next two steps are rightful action and livelihood. These include the things a person does on the day-to-day, including their job and profession. A person should be active, working, and in a job where they're not gaming or scheming. It goes without saying that they should not be working at anything illegal. This matches the above where Jesus told people to do their job, do it well, treat people fairly in it, and to "be content with your pay."

Effort, mindfulness, and concentration would be the next three ways Buddha would recommend working at or on being happy. What a person thinks about and dwells on will be what a person does. It will determine how they act, especially towards others. These three very much contain elements of 'do unto others,' 'do no harm,' and non-attachment. Obsessing over something, even someone, will lead to anything from fear, to control, to lies, and more. It will very much lead to the opposite of happiness. An unattached and peaceful mind frees a person to take and enjoy things as they come and then let go when things change. The signature response in this scenario is gratitude for blessings received, and in some cases, things not received, i.e. 'better off without them' kinds of things. In either case the idea is to be appreciative instead of jealous and bitter.

Buddha's last two suggestions for leading a happy, enlightened life are to have right views and intentions. These again determine one's actions. A person's views and intentions will be obvious from what they do. If they have harmony and balance in their lives they will live in peace with self and others. If they are living self-centeredly their lives will be full of vanity, pride, fear, anger, jealousy, hate, etc.

Buddha's recommendations lead to happiness and the karma of positive actions and results in this life, the by-passing of reincarnation, and the moving on to Nirvana in the next. Jesus' recommendations lead to a happy, blessed life of "Your kingdom come, your will be done, on Earth as it is in Heaven." Once such a life here on Earth is done, the person by-passes Purgatory/Hell and moves on to Heaven. Jesus' and Buddha's plans are remarkably similar then. Both of them even have eight steps.

9 - Hell and Samsara

Recently Pope Francis of the Catholic Church caused a media blitz in the religious and non-religious world alike when he supposedly told a reporter that there is no literal Hell. Hell is figurative and simple metaphor for 'separation from God' he said, according to the reporter. The story later proved false as the Pope was misquoted, but it did bring back into focus what is oftentimes a conundrum for Christians, especially when trying to explain their faith to other cultures: how can there be both an All-kind, All-loving, All-good God, *and* a Hell?

Jesus said in Matt. 25:41 that Hell was created "for the Devil and his angels." Why then, are *people* sent there? The preacher down at the corner church will likely say "God doesn't send people to Hell; they choose it!" Ok fine, but Jesus told Peter we were to forgive each other not just seven times but seven times seven (49 times), and that for the same single offense (Matt. 18:22).[32] Some translations have this at 'seventy *plus* seven' (77 times),

---

[32] In the OT forgiving a person and/or remitting their debt once every seven years was considered the standard of mercy. The seventh year in a cycle was called 'The Year of Jubilee' because of this. Peter had asked if seven times as

others at 'seventy *times* seven' (490 times!). In other words, according to Jesus, there should be no limit to our forgiveness. If *we* were/are supposed to have unlimited forgiveness, wouldn't *God*?

If a person sins during their seventy-something years on Earth, maybe even often, maybe even seriously, maybe even often *and* seriously, why are they sent to Hell instead of simply being forgiven? If very few people are born inherently evil, then most of a person's sins are likely due to their circumstances. Wouldn't God take this into account? If they *are* sent to Hell, how long do they have to stay? Would they 'burn in Hell' for seventy years, seventy pus seven years, seventy times seven years, seven hundred years, seven thousand years, or simply *forever*? On the other hand, if time as a thing doesn't exist in Hell and there is only one continuous and unending moment, does subjecting a person to just such a moment of agonizing pain and terror, reconcile with an All-loving, All-forgiving God? [33]

---

much forgiveness was sufficient, and after that hold the person accountable. Jesus instead introduced here a whole new standard: unlimited forgiveness.

[33] A way to think about this might be to find oneself waking up in Hell at 12:00:00, in terrible pain and agony, and the clock never ticking to 12:00:01.

Assuming a person did deserve to go to Hell, wouldn't their time in Hell, at least at some point, be done?[34] Even if there's a defiantly bitter and unrepentant sinner who in Hell only and spitefully 'gnashes their teeth at God' (Matt. 13:42), wouldn't it be better, more humane, *even more economical*, to simply 'extinguish them?'[35]

For these and other reasons many people within Christianity today no longer believe in a literal Hell. As an adult Bible-school teacher I found this to be increasingly the case over the past twenty-five years. I especially found it to be so when I researched for my book *Hell in the Bible*. Sometimes it is their official belief, but for many it is kind of an 'unofficial' belief; that God would never really send anyone to Hell. "You have this life to get it right" more than a few people have told me. "If you do, you go to Heaven. If you don't, there's nothing" they added. The belief that this life is a preparation for the next would not be dissimilar from Buddhism. As a minimum, the belief that the works of this life *play out* in this life would not be dissimilar from Buddhism.

---

[35] While Aristotle was ambivalent as to whether any souls ever make it to a nether region after exiting the body, he was very clear that a particularly bad person's soul was totally extinguished at death. They were snuffed out like a candle, and any components were 'dispersed to the winds' (Aristotle's *Metaphysics*).

"*This* world, *this* life, is the only Hell there is" is another comment I've heard may times over the years. The idea here is that the trials and tribulations and *sufferings* of this life are a Hell of sorts. This of course would be compatible with Buddhism. There would be both the idea of suffering *in* this life and that *this* life is where you suffer; not Hell. Although limited to only one life, there would still be a Samsara (reincarnation cycle) nature to this in that you have "this life to get it right." Any particular life a person may be on at the time *is* 'this life.' The 'getting it right' takes place here and not in an afterlife of punishment. 'Accounts are settled' and 'debts are paid,' as it were, in this life now and through the very karmic idea that 'you reap what you sow.'[36]

Again and as above, Purgatory provides another meeting point between a Christian Hell and a Buddhist Samsara in that while the person's soul may not be recycling back into this world per se, it isn't leaving either. It stays here, somehow here but not quite here, to observe, learn, and be purified. This purification may involve pain or even a 'burning away' of sin/sin nature, but only to the extent that it prepares the person for Heaven.[37] The idea here is

---

[36] This is a Christian notion found in both the OT and NT and perhaps most notably expressed by Paul in Gal. 6:7.
[37] 1st Cor. 3:12-15 is often pointed to as a scriptural reference for Purgatory.

that a person can be forgiven, but this doesn't make them pure or holy, and nothing and unholy or impure can enter Heaven (Rev.21:27). Seen in this light then, Purgatory is again part of a preparation process for Heaven and therefore of benefit to people who go there. Purgatory would not last forever, neither is it said that anyone ever 'fails' Purgatory. No one is ever said to go from Purgatory to Hell, as this would be a step in the wrong direction. With Purgatory if there is not the idea of 'recycling' there is at least the idea of 'cycling' or processing or perfecting of a soul so that it can proceed to a final place of rest and bliss. Though not expressed in exactly the same way as Buddhism, the basic components are nonetheless still there.

The long-standing pop culture belief in 'ghosts,' even among church-goers, could be said to be due in part to a reaction to the idea of a Hell. While the subject of ghosts has traditionally been linked by the Church to OT prohibitions against witchcraft and 'necromancy,' Church teachings today vary from one group to the next.[38] More fundamental groups deny ghosts altogether, while other groups might simply say it's an unknown or at least 'gray area.'[39] Those who deny any kind of lingering spirits would say then that

---

[38] Necromancy is the belief in, study of, and consultation with 'spirits of the dead' i.e. ghosts.
[39] For a thorough and scriptural study on the subject of ghosts, please see my book *Demons in the Bible*.

'this life is all there is.' The person has this life to get it right. This would be similar to a 'once-thru' Samsara. Those who allow for some kind of lingering spirits, who remain for time to settle 'unfinished business,' would be thinking along the lines of a post-life Samsara/Purgatory type process. Those who simply say it is all an unknown would be in agreement with the essentials of Buddha's no-soul concept, and that as a minimum (without enlightenment) flesh-and-blood persons can have no knowledge of how things work outside our physical world and realm.

The point here is that in any of the above positions, people in the West, in and out of Church, already show movement towards at least some kind of Purgatory if not some kind of Samsara, and away from the idea that Hell is a given and absolute: a place of eternal punishment for all sinners, regardless of type or amount of their sin, and not offset by, any kind of redeeming works they may have done during their life.[40] With all this being especially true for all those not Christian, which of course would be almost all the people who have ever lived, now and in the past.[41]

---

[40] For a thorough and scriptural study on the subject of Hell, please see my book *Hell in the Bible*.

[41] Christianity has been on the scene for some 2000 years; scientists think people have been on the scene for 150, 000 years. This means humanity has only had Christianity for .0003% of its history. Said another way, 99.9997% of human history there has been neither the choice nor chance to *be* Christian.

Interestingly enough, in Buddhism there is in fact a Hell. It is called 'Naraka' and is also thought to be deep inside the Earth.[42] As opposed to it being a place of fire though, it is thought to be a place of extreme cold. People also are not *sent* there at death but are rather *reborn* there as living but spiritual residents, and as part of a 'last effort' to redeem them when previous incarnations failed to yield enlightenment. It is a place of punishment but a place where the punishment is seen less as revenge than it is 'reconditioning.' The time is fixed, not limitless, and based on the person's misdeeds of the previous life, with any good they did factored in.

In addition, the living back home on Earth may pray for those in Naraka, that their time there may be reduced. The living may even volunteer to take on some of their punishment, which in turn counts as good karma for the living. Catholics readers will of course recognize this as a very Catholic

---

Either Hell is completely full with all of these or it isn't. If it isn't then God accepts other paths. Hell might not automatically be a sentence for almost everyone as soon as they're born, and Heaven may have more in it than the members of 'such-and-such' congregation from 'such-and-such' denomination from 'such-and-such' wing of Christianity.

[42] The traditional location of Hell was thought to be in underground caverns deep inside the Earth, based on certain OT verses and especially due to influences from the Greek idea of 'Hades': a generic and underground 'realm of the dead.'

practice, that of praying for souls in Purgatory. Many Catholic churches even have 'Purgatory Societies,' where groups of people meet once a week to pray for any 'lost souls.' 'Prayers for the dead' are also a regular feature of Catholic weekly masses, wherein the congregation asks that any souls not yet advanced on to Heaven may be able to do so. In either the Christian Purgatory or the Buddhist Naraka there is then the idea that *neither* last forever: people go there for a time, for 'perfecting,' and eventually do get out. The Christian would go on to Heaven: the Buddhist on to Nirvana.

The pivotal question in all of this, in attempting to reconcile an All-forgiving God with Hell, and comparing to Samsara/Naraka, might lie then not with whether Hell *exists* but whether it is *eternal*.

Rev. 20:12-15 has some interesting light to shed on the subject. In a scene commonly referred to as 'the Great White Throne Judgment,' Hell 'gives up its dead' and is emptied out, the residents of which stand before God for a judgment. 'Books are opened' and anyone "who is not found in the Book of Life" is dispatched to the "Lake of Fire," which *is* said to be or last "forever and ever."

There are several notable take-a-ways from this scene. The first and most basic is that the Lake of Fire and Hell are not the same thing. The Lake of Fire is in a different location and larger than Hell, as Hell is moved there and 'thrown in' (vs. 14). Another is that this appears to make the Lake of Fire eternal but Hell not. Another, and most importantly for this discussion, is that there is a judgment of *those in Hell prior to 'the throwing.'* While it could be that this is simply a formality and re-rendering of a 'guilty' verdict, this seems a waste. Why create a new place for souls to burn when there's an existing place where souls are already burning? Why go through some type of trial or judging, only to rule 'still guilty' on all residents, and then transfer them from one place of fire to another place of fire?

Verse 15's "If anyone's name was not found in the Book of Life they were thrown into the fire," suggests that there may be some from this crowd whose names *are* in the book. If not 'innocent' or 'reformed' then perhaps at least 'time served' and no longer deserving of fire or 'the Second Death.' The fact that this Lake of Fire judgment is called 'the Second Death' suggests something more than a continuation of burning. Some have argued this indicates annihilation, where the soul is disintegrated, dispersed, or otherwise broken down, and the *components* are what burn forever. This is the fate of the Devil and his angels, and they were already in Hell too, but would the souls of *people* warrant the same fate?

If so, then one is left with the question of "How many lifetimes does a person have to suffer, for the sins of one lifetime?" There would only be left the preacher on the corner's answer that while seeming to be unfair, "They chose it!" If on the other hand, there is an actual judgment happening in this scene, it moves the seeming contradiction of an All-forgiving God and a Hell towards some kind of reconciliation, *and* closer to a Buddhist notion of these things.

The next chapter, Rev. 21, provides additional hints. In describing 'the New Jerusalem' that has come down from Heaven and wherein all saints now dwell, John pauses twice to point out that 'no one impure or shameful' can ever enter or go in. This is supposedly after Hell has been done away with and its former residents (or their components) have all been moved to the Lake of Fire and are all now in there and burning. At this point there should be no one left or around other than former residents of Heaven. If this is the case, why mention that there may be some on hand that while in the vicinity of the city, can't go in? Is this simply a reverse way of saying, twice, that all people there *are* pure and holy because they are *not* impure or unholy? Why not just say "all people around there are pure and holy, and everyone goes in!"? This may be splitting hairs, but John's curious wording here seems to at least open the possibility that at the above judgment, some people actually got judged, and it was with something more than a 'still guilty' or 'they've burned, now let their components burn' verdict. This in turn might provide some resolution for all those mentioned at the top who find the existence of a one-size-fits all Hell that lasts forever to be inequitable.

Much time and space has been spent here because the final dispensation of souls is what is ostensibly one of the greatest disconnects between Christianity and Buddhism: do souls come back, or do they move on? If they move on, is there punishment (or at least reconditioning), and if there is, for how long? With above ideas such as 'having this life to get it right,' there being both a Purgatory *and* a Hell, neither of which are forever (the former of which processes people on to Heaven, the latter of which processes people out of the penal system), the two faiths are closer in this area than it might initially seem.

10 - Heaven and Nirvana

In Christianity there is a thought to be a spiritual realm or plane, where good, redeemed, and saved people go at death. God resides and has a throne there. Jesus lives there. Angels and various celestial beings live there.[43] A person's dearly departed friends and relatives are there. Their pets may even be there.[44]

In Heaven people are conscious and awake. They are aware of themselves and others and thought to have preternatural characteristics. They are out of the body and in spirit form. They are not in pain. There is no more suffering (Rev. 21:4). While it is unclear from scripture what all they *do* once there (besides being 'not in pain'), it is clear that at least *some* of this involves rest,

---

[43] Heaven also hosts the 'twenty-four elders,' the 'four living beings,' and the 'two witnesses' (Rev. 4:4, Rev. 5:14, and Rev. 11:3 respectively). These may be angels in the traditional sense or some other type of celestial being. In its broadest sense and translation angel simply means 'celestial being' or 'being from the heavenlies,' so this could mean almost anything. Either way there appears to be more than one kind of angel and/or celestial being in Heaven. For a thorough and scriptural study of angels, please my book *Angels in the Bible*.

[44] As to whether there are animals in Heaven please see 2nd Ki. 6:17 and Rev. 19:14.

a state of joy/bliss, praying for those back on Earth, and communing with God (Matt. 25:21, 2nd Thess. 1:7, Rev. 8:3, et al). Jesus said people there become like angels in their relationship with God (Matt. 22:30). While *none* of this involves sitting on clouds or playing harps, apparently *some* of it involves mansions, crowns, and robes (Jn. 14:2, 2nd Tim. 4:8, Rev. 6:11).[45] Much of this also appears to involve being grateful, and in a constant state of worship (Rev. 5:12). Essential basics then of a Christian Heaven are that people there are changed, and can see, know, and be with God, in a new/superior way. And that as a place Heaven is invisible, non-corporeal, and 'somewhere else.' Almost everyone would agree that *somewhere* is, if nothing else, 'up.'

Buddha would draw off his Hindu background when thinking about his version of Heaven, or Nirvana. He agreed that it is another place, another realm, on another plane, and full of supernatural beings.[46] Hinduism teaches that life has just kind of always been here, and that there never was a place

---

[45] There are no scriptural precedents for people in Heaven sitting on clouds and playing harps, or 'getting wings.' This is pop culture tradition.

[46] As mentioned above, Buddha claimed the role of Supreme Being for himself. While this may seem a bit 'over the top' to some, it's important to note that Jesus himself claimed to be 'one with the Father' and as such equal with God (Jn. 10:30). The Nicaean Creed says that Jesus is "consubstantial with the Father."

or time of a *beginning*.⁴⁷ When people die, if not reincarnated they become part of a generic life force, something most readers would probably liken to 'the Force' in 'Star Wars.' Buddhism embraces this too. When Buddha died followers believed he became part of this same force, and went on to/attained Nirvana. He became the 'Cosmic Buddha.' He exists in some kind of universal out-of-the-body, superior consciousness. In temples his symbol is a simple circle, placed against a plain or empty background. This indicates completeness and fullness, but also emptiness and nothingness.

When Buddhists use words like 'empty', 'nothing,' 'cessation,' etc., to talk about Nirvana, persons in the West will likely think they are speaking only about the finality of the grave, the solace of death. Nirvana in this sense, would be no more than 'they can't hurt you anymore,' which would be much less than, and far removed from the Christian notion of Heaven and/or life after death in general. In Christianity there is a strong sense of 'settling accounts,' as it were, and this requires that a person continues to live, in

---

⁴⁷ The Greeks struggled with this idea for some time too, calling it 'infinite regression.' Thinkers such as Aristotle ultimately concluded that one could not just keep going endlessly backwards to various points and always find something there. At some point, they said, there had to be a 'nothing prior' (a priori), which would also simultaneously be the beginning. Whoever/Whatever initiated the beginning Aristotle and others referred to as 'the Prime Mover.' Ibid.

some way, so as to be able to receive (and know they're receiving) their just dues. In Buddhism the choices might appear to be, to someone from the West, the finality of the grave, or reincarnation (where the person has no memory of previous lives), or turning into a generic life force. Any of these might seem to circumnavigate a reward/punishment system.

In the Buddhist sense however, life never really ends, ceases, or goes away: It continually recycles and always has/always will. Nirvana is the cessation of the recycling, according to the way we understand recycling. Empty, nothing, cessation, etc., seen in this sense simply means the end of 'life as we know it,' in favor of something we do not and cannot know. Since all our knowledge come from the physics of the corporeal, we have no real way to talk or even think about such a place. For the Buddhist if a physical world is constantly changing, and this causes suffering, Nirvana, as a non-physical realm, would be 'not that.' Physics, at least as we know them, would not apply. As such there would be no motion, no action/reaction, no karma, no attachments, no suffering. There would be only the purity and bliss of unfettered, *completely unfettered*, life and living, and of being a part of *life itself* as a thing. Reward/punishment in this system are shoved to the background in favor of living, and that to a cessation of *living as we know it.*

This may sound a bit better to the Christian, but there would still seem to be an issue with Buddhism's lack of separate and distinct and personal identities in the next life. It is suggestive of some kind of 'one,' or 'one-ness,' or 'becoming one' with nature, the world, life itself, or even God. This is problematic until we read of Jesus offering one of his last prayers, a prayer of unity or even oneness, for his Disciples:

> "I have revealed you to those whom you gave me out of the world. They were yours; you gave them to me and they have obeyed your word...Now they know that everything you have given me comes from you...For I gave them the words you gave me and they accepted them. They knew with certainty that I came from you, and they believed that you sent me...All I have is yours, and all you have is mine. And glory has come to me through them...I will remain in the world no longer, but they are still in the world...I am coming to you...protect them...so that they may be one as we are one...I am coming to you now, but I say these things while I am still in the world, so that they may have the full measure of my joy within them...I have given them your word and the world has hated them, for they are not of the world any more than I am of the world...They are not of the world, even as I am not of it...For them I sanctify myself, that they too may be truly sanctified...My prayer is not for

them alone. I pray also for those who will believe in me through their message, that all of them may be one, Father, just as you are in me and I am in you…May they also be in us…I have given them the glory that you gave me, that they may be one as we are one— I in them and you in me—so that they may be brought to complete unity…Then the world will know that you sent me and have loved them even as you have loved me…Father, I want those you have given me to be with me where I am…Righteous Father, though the world does not know you, I know you, and they know that you have sent me…I have made you known to them, and will continue to make you known in order that the love you have for me may be in them and that I myself may be in them." (John 17).[48]

All of this "I in you and you in me and I in them and them in me and us in them and them in us" sounds like much more than a generic message of church unity: in fact it sounds an awful lot like *one-ness*. It sounds like maintaining distinct identities yet being one at the same time. If Buddha became the Cosmic Buddha and became something else, some part of life itself (and that on a higher plane), and yet maintained his identity and consciousness - to the point of being able to hear and respond to prayers -

---

[48] Selected highlights mine.

then all that Buddhism is really saying is just what Jesus asked for here too; that he and followers may go to some kind of next level state of completeness, fullness, and one-ness. If this is Nirvana it sounds an awful lot like Heaven.

In any case, the net take-a-ways from both Heaven and Nirvana would at a minimum be that both are invisible, non-corporeal, spiritual, supernatural realms where people are together with each other and God.[49] Things work differently there than here on Earth. There is bliss and rest, and completeness in both. There is life in both and cessation in both in that in both that there is no more 'becoming' in either: both are forever.

---

[49] The reader will have to decide their own definition as to 'together' i.e. simply in the presence of, or at one with.

11 - Buddhism and Me

From 2008 to 2015 I experienced major upheavals in my life. To say that 'there was change' would be an *understatement,* at the least. During that seven year stretch I lost Mom and Dad, my marriage, my job, my home and two dogs. My kids, who had always been my closest friends and support group, all got married during this same period and moved away, some out-of-state. I moved away too in an effort to start over, and found myself a hundred miles away from my previous environs. I was essentially home alone and in my 50's and starting over as if I were 18. I had hope for some kind of a new beginning when I met a wonderful woman during this period and we got engaged. However, one month before our wedding she passed away too.

Needless to say all this change, coming in so many waves and yet at what seemed like all at once, left me feeling shell-shocked. All my tether points, all the things I was used to, all the *people* I was used to, were gone just gone. This included church. At the beginning of this period I was very active in my local church, a Church of Christ spin-off called 'such-and-such Christian Church.' I weekly taught, spoke, and sang (as part of a choir, a group, or as a soloist). As some of the changes in my situation began to be rumored about, especially as to my marriage, I noticed a change in the way people at church acted towards me. There was sympathy but also avoidance. It was like I had something they didn't want to catch. I also especially noticed that beyond some of the people, some of the time, telling me that I was in their 'thoughts and prayers,' the wheels at church never really stopped or paused on my account. It was for the most part each week business as usual, and if there were any problem members present the crowd simply looked the other way.

Prior to all these changes I had however, went back to school to finish my degree and studied Christianity and the NT in a formal and academic setting. Early on it became apparent that the early Church, from the first century, through the early Church Fathers and beyond, looked extremely Catholic. The writings, the language, the symbolism; it all seemed like visiting with a local Catholic Priest. There seemed to be one official way to do things, as to teachings and liturgies and structure and authority, and *especially* Eucharist. The various denominational groups with which I'd been familiar stood apart from this tradition and history.

One might reasonably ask the question "Yeah, but isn't it OK, even a good thing, to start new and different churches?" According to early writings the answer was an emphatic "No!" They were extremely protective of the beliefs, practices, doctrines, etc., that had been passed down from the original Apostles, men who had actually 'been with the Lord,' and not open to other versions. In fact, other versions were frequently referred to as 'heresies' in early Church writings. This meant my churches, the ones I'd went to over the years, were not part of the actual, authentic, historic stream. They were much later break-a-ways and start-ups, usually based on a founder's dream or vision, and were utterly lacking in tradition, history, and scriptural authority. This seemed odd since almost all of them claimed to be 'Bible-only' churches who only went by the Bible, but weren't going by it. Many even tried to use the Bible to counter or 'disprove' Catholicism. A daunting task to say the least, if in fact not fantasy (or in today's lingo 'fake news'), since the Bible came from the Catholic Church in 325 A.D. via the Council of Nicaea. It struck me that this would be rather like a local car repair shop trying to argue repair manual details with the car's designers back in Detroit: those who built the car and wrote the manual!

In any event, my prior private at-home study of scripture combined with my new academic study started me on an inexorable journey towards Catholicism. Initially I thought I would just stay Protestant and practice my Catholicism in secret. I thought I could be a 'Closet Catholic,' and share some of my new-found information with my fellows via my teaching, speaking, and singing.[50] [51] At my church they also had a 'Communion talk' each week before people received 'the Lord's Supper.' I frequently did this too, and once in school began to share some of what I'd learned about communion, i.e. that the early Church had considered it the actual body and blood of Christ. I even backed up my talks with scriptures, especially John 6. While the members were very receptive to all this, I could tell from the frowns on the faces of the Elders and Deacons that the walls there at church would soon be closing in on me. When the next quarterly speaker schedule came out I noticed I wasn't on it. I was also told the various classes I was leading or teaching on Sunday mornings and Wednesday nights were not being 'renewed.' The students were to be 'absorbed' by other classes. I was no longer on the singing schedule either, in any capacity. When I inquired as to what happened, each person I asked (each of whom were *exactly* in charge of the scheduling) said "I don't know!" If accident or error it was never fixed,

---

[50] For my conversion to Catholicism story, please see my book *A Closet Catholic Comes Out, and Avoids the Cafeteria*.

[51] The 'Cafeteria' in my book's title refers to the slang belief that many Catholics today are 'Cafeteria Catholics': they pick and choose which teachings they want to follow, as if they were going through a cafeteria line. I had just come from a world of Protestantism where there were as many teachings on any set issue as there were interpretations of the verse upon which the teaching was supposedly based. I didn't want a repeat of that.

and I stayed 'dis-invited' from my previous roles. The message was received and 'that was that' for my attempt at being a Closet Catholic.

As all of this latter went down just before my move, once I moved I decided to look into Catholicism in earnest. I found a local Catholic church and asked, "How do I join?" They put me in an 'R.C.I.A.' class.[52] Early on in these classes I noticed something present that had been missing in my former church(es): teachings on and about suffering. In the Protestant church the idea had been that God blesses his people, according to the way that most people think of blessings: good times, health, money, etc.[53] There really was no room for suffering in this equation. If there was suffering, it was assumed there must be a problem, and that on the part of the individual. The person 'lacked the faith' necessary to simply 'accept and receive' God's blessings, or, they were perhaps living in 'disobedience' i.e. sin. To plug back into the blessings stream the answer seemed obvious: increase faith and stop

---

[52] Non-Catholic adults who wish to become Catholic are required to go through a 'Rite of Christian Initiation for Adults' class where they are taught about the Catholic Church. It typically lasts one year. Persons can only 'join' the Catholic Church via this process, which culminates with the annual Easter Vigil. This is the Saturday night service the night before Easter morning, and is the biggest service of the year for Catholics. RCIA candidates 'graduate,' and are 'received into the Church' on this night.

[53] I had long taught against this, and while some people called it a 'health and prosperity' doctrine, I frequently referred to it as a gospel of 'candy, popcorn, and Coca-Cola.'

sinning. I found this to have very much been the mindset of the congregations and preachers I'd known over the years, especially as things had started to go south for me. At a minimum some preacher friends had told me in confidence, "Well Y'know Sonny, we just figure in such situations that there's *something* going on and it's none of our business."

I guessed this was a fair enough assessment, but I also found it to be shallow. It was an easy way out, easy for them, and required little or no effort on their part. They never knew if I might have been receptive to some kind of help or at least counseling, as no one, not the ministers or the elders or the deacons or even fellow churchmen, ever stopped by or even called. And this was all during and *post* arrival of an 'information age' where there were 1001 new and different and *instant ways* to connect with people. In any case and be that as it may, I'd experienced no real teaching on suffering in these churches other than again, it being sort of like a disease, and one where the person was better off avoided.

In the Catholic Church however, I was learning that suffering was believed to have a purpose and could even be a part of God's plan. It might be for anything from some type of trial or testing, to reproof/correction, to even a putting on the living the sins (at least *some* sins) of those in Purgatory/Hell.[54] Any of these, especially the last, were viewed as blessings by Catholics. The idea of a 'blessing' included more than whatever profited a person materially now. This was especially noticeable when I heard how Catholics prayed. Whereas I was used to lengthy prayers where we named people, listed all their issues to God, and then gave God all *our* recommended solutions (we of course backed up this prayer model with scripture, and even quoted/cited certain verses back to God!), Catholics simply mentioned large groups of people ('all those sick,' 'all those traveling,' 'those in nursing homes,' etc.) and said, "We pray to the Lord." This was spoken by the prayer leader, usually the priest, to which the congregation simply answered back "Lord, here our prayer."[55] The specific details were all left up to God, and this included the possibility that there might be suffering.

Although I missed the suffering connection to Buddhism I did get that this was a completely different take on suffering *and* prayer than what I'd been used to in my previous churches. To be honest, it seemed more realistic, if

---

[54] I was unaware at the time of how much some of this, especially the latter, had in common with Buddhism.

[55] For the longest time in I would turn to a neighbor afterwards and say "Lord hear our prayer? What prayer? We didn't ask for anything!" Old-school Catholics refer to this type of praying as 'offering it up.' You list generic non-specific prayer requests, or 'intentions,' and simply 'leave them with God.'

not more honest or even refreshing. Taken together with what I'd already been studying in school as to the Early Church, I 'came home' as they say, finished RCIA and converted. I was received into the Church on Easter Vigil 2012.

Becoming Catholic was a huge game changer for me. It answered many of my questions, solved many of my doctrinal issues, and allowed me to begin to establish new tether and anchor points. It allowed me to cope with the changes in my life, to 'trust and obey' God, and move on. It did not however, go to quieting the 'voices' in my head. I once heard Dr. James Dobson say that any adult male's identity and feelings of self-worth are linked to, and wrapped up in and around his job, his home, and his wife.[56] I had lost all three. I dealt daily with a constant inner monologue which *criticized* me for being retired while at the same time saying that whatever else I might be involved in was *worthless* because I was single.[57] I had always dealt with

---

[56] Dr. James Dobson is a well-known Christian psychologist, author, speaker, and long-time host of the syndicated radio show 'Focus on the Family.'
[57] The company at which I'd been for nearly 30 years was sold to an out-of-state conglomerate that wanted our brand and our customers, but not our local manufacturing plant. They already had multiple and newer facilities. Shutdown procedures for our plant took a couple of years, and during that time older employees took early retirement so younger employees could work a little longer. I was one of the former. My inner voice took turns telling me I was *guilty* for not staying (even though the plant was closing), and *lazy* for retiring.

feelings of guilt, but now even more so. This played out in the everyday in that if I cleaned house or cut grass or went to the grocery or went out to eat and then shopping, or whatever, I would hear a nagging "You don't deserve this" coming from inside my head. At the same time, especially if it had been a particularly *good* day, I would hear "Yeah, but so what? You ain't got nobody!"

For the longest time I assumed this had something to do with sin. Much of today's Protestant world, especially the fundamental and evangelical wings, are rooted in and descended from the teachings of John Calvin, who said that all men are inherently evil and 'absolutely depraved.'[58] Everyone, according to Calvin, is a sinner who deserves to go to Hell. This was my background as well, and I figured the accusing voice in my head must have been something like a guilty conscious. It was 'calling me to repent,' which I did a lot of, sometimes unsure of exactly what I'd done and knowing only that I was guilty.

---

[58] Calvinism teaches five central doctrinal points: (t)otal depravity of man, (u)nconditional election, (l)imited atonement, (i)rresistible grace, and (p)erseverance of the saints. This is sometimes called 'the Tulip Doctrine.'

Now as a Catholic, I had the additional resource of the confessional booth. Catholics stress sin too, but perhaps emphasize the love and forgiveness and acceptance of God a bit more than do Protestants. Although many Catholics, especially 'Cradle Catholics,' avoid confession and see it as outdated and even a hassle, I embraced it and went every week.[59] I often didn't have anything real to confess other than I seemed to feel guilty all the time, and that perhaps I 'needed more faith.' The priest would always listen, absolve me of my sins, and then usually say something like 'God forgives you, I forgive you, make sure *YOU* forgive you.'

During one of these sessions a visiting priest listened for a while and then interrupted me: "Sonny, did you have abusive or overbearing parents? It's not normal for a normal, regular person to have this much guilt." I was taken aback, didn't really know what to say, and don't remember how the rest of the confession went. I'm sure he absolved me, and I just went on from there and into mass. I did however, earmark and footnote his remarks. At the same time while confession helped some with the guilt problem, it did not address the unworthiness component of "You ain't got nobody!"

---

[59] 'Cradle Catholic' is a slang term for persons born into a Catholic family and raised their whole life as a Catholic.

While all this was going on I was now retired and wanted to stay busy. I'd always heard that after major change(s) it helps to stay busy, and I'd always liked school. I'd finished my degree in religion a few years prior and now found myself wanting to go back and study something similar, but in a slightly different field. Now living in a different state I would be going to a different school, which I thought might be kind of refreshing and nice. I met with some of the advisors, and after talking with them about my background and current interests, they suggested I pursue a degree in philosophy, but in disciplines other than those of the West. A couple classes in, I discovered Buddhism.

Buddha introduced me to concepts like attachment and the no-self. Buddha said that of all creatures in the animal kingdom, humans are the only ones that can conceptualize their situation and 'think outside the box.'[60] By this he meant that of all living creatures, people are the only ones, who if they have a bowl of food in front to them, will launch into inner monologue instead of just eating it and being happy. People use memory and experience, combined with desire, imagination, and *fear,* to form judgments

---

[60] My paraphrasing.

about the food. This is so as to try and somehow *control,* or at least *predict,* both the food *and* the future. A person might ask:

"Where did this food come from?"

"Why is it here?"

"What is it made of?"

"What does it taste like?"

"Could it be made to taste better?"

"How long will it last?"

"Should I eat it all now or save some?"

"Should I share it?"

"Should I keep it?"

"I wonder if my neighbor has food?"

"I wonder if my neighbor has more/better food than me?"

"Should I try and take my neighbor's food?"

"I wonder if my neighbor knows I have *this* food?"

"What if my neighbor tries to take *my* food?"

"Should I fear my neighbor?"

All of this takes place within the first few moments of seeing the food. Even after eating the food though, the obsessing continues:

"Ok I ate it and it was good and I don't feel guilty. But I ate alone."

Buddha said this was all an attachment issue, and while there may be other persons, places, and things involved, ultimately what any person is really attached to is *themselves*: an idealized, unrealized, *unattainable* version of self. People don't like change, and this agonizing over one's situation is an attempt to see if one is 'OK' and either has or can get some kind of imagined control of things. This game plan is however, all theoretical and hypothetical. It has no form or matter. It does not exist in time and space. It is nothing more than a speculative version of one's self and circumstances, based again on senses, memory, imagination and especially *fear*. Everyone goes by it, tries to please it, and finds themselves answering to it. This is again, a situation unique to people. No other animals do it, but all people do it.

This idea of answering to someone who wasn't there was new to me. In fact it was revelatory. I had gotten pretty good at out arguing the voices when they said I was guilty/worthless, but I was still having to argue. This new dynamic switched the topic from the argument to the voice itself, *and Buddha was telling me the voice didn't exist.*

I began to look back at my life and noticed that even before the recent troubles, I'd always had these feelings and heard these voices. At some point I paused to ask myself "When was the last time you didn't feel guilty?" In less than a second I blurted out "Well, never!" When I was working I always felt guilty that I'd not finished school and gone to a different career. Back in the day, when I was a full-time student, I felt guilty that I wasn't working since all my other friends seemed to have money. When I was married I felt guilty for not being able to provide a better lifestyle for my family.[61] As my marriage started to come apart I thought it was all my fault and felt guilty. I wondered if I should've just stayed single, or what it would be like to now be single and felt guilty for that. I'd never been popular at work, I'd never been popular at school, I'd never been popular in any neighborhood. I thought all was my fault. I'd been scrawny as a kid and was picked on and bullied a lot. I came from a poor family and was made fun of for that. I felt like my mom and dad had always resented me, and that they thought they could have had a better life had I not been born. They would have had more money and more opportunity. Dad especially, would not have been forced to work at a place he hated for all those years, in order to raise and support me.

As the list was going on and on the priest's comments from earlier suddenly came back to mind: "Sonny, did you have abusive or overbearing

---

[61] To be sure, we had a fairly standard middle-class lifestyle, but I felt like I owed my family more as measured against some ideal but imaginary standard.

parents?" Now it all made sense. I'd been dealing my whole life with psychological issues, with issues and ideas about self, that had been formed in me early, and which had only been added to as the years went on. If something negative happened I blamed myself and felt guilty. If I saw other people and their better situation, I felt insufficient and again, unworthy. If people put me down, made fun of me, criticized me, etc., I thought I deserved it and that they were probably right and added another layer on to the whole deal: *to self.*

I'd been buying into something however, that was not real, and even if any of it had been real, it was all in the past. It could no longer get me. The Christian take on all this was to 'forgive and forget' or to 'forgive and let go.' Here Buddha was now in front of me saying that there was nothing to let go: it was not real and never existed in the first place. It was all impressions and take-a-ways and voices I'd coalesced and personified into a *self.* I did not think of this self as me, but I did feel like I had to answer to it. Buddha was telling me I didn't have to answer to it, that it was all 'mist and vapor;' less than mist and vapor. It was nothing. *There was no such person, identity, or self.*

To say all this was liberating, to say all this was freeing, would be the greatest of understatements. In fact it was nothing short of a 'born-again' type experience. I'd been born-again or 'saved' (in the Christian sense) when I was 16.[62] This was like a second born-again experience. For some reason another quote came into my mind. It was, of all things, a line from one of the *Star Wars* movies. An older Jedi master advises a younger Jedi, "Don't center on your anxieties, keep your focus on the here-and-now, where it belongs."[63] To not do so, to spend all your time thinking and obsessing about self, was not only misguided but selfish and self-centered. This was certainly the opposite of what Jesus taught, but because of attempting to filter everything through sin/no sin, I'd somehow missed this point.[64] Another Star Wars line

---

[62] Much of the Evangelical line of Christianity cites John 3:3-8 as scriptural precedent for the idea of a sudden conversion experience, usually done at an altar call at the front of, and in front of, a congregation, wherein a person 'accepts Jesus Christ as their personal Savior' and is suddenly, instantly 'saved.' Here 'saved' means pardoned and no longer guilty and deserving of Hell, which again as per Calvinism, is most people's fate.

[63] Star Wars fans will recognize this as a comment from Qui-Gon Jinn to a younger Obi-Wan Kenobi in "Star Wars: The Phantom Menace."

[64] Paul does perhaps the best job of explaining Jesus' teaching on self and self-centeredness when he says in Phi. 2:5-8 "Make your own attitude that of Christ Jesus, who existing in the form of God, did not consider equality with God as something to be used for His own advantage. Instead He emptied Himself by assuming the form of a slave, taking on the likeness of men. And when He had come as a man in His external form, He humbled Himself by becoming obedient to the point of death." This is an ultimate expressing of putting others first and not being consumed with self, whether that be enhancing/improving ones's station in life or *constantly judging/criticizing self*. This latter is maybe worse because it is neither attainable nor even

suddenly came to mind; "Fear leads to anger, anger leads to hate, hate leads to suffering."[65] Everything was becoming clear. By submitting to the leadership, guidance, and judgement of self, because of fear, I'd wound up hating myself. I never wanted to hurt myself, but I'd had a low opinion of myself, going all the way back. The mental energy required to be in constant internal debate with self, in order to somehow justify self to self, was overwhelmingly taxing and mind-numbing. As it left no room to think about others and their situation, it bordered on a type of narcissism.

Thanks to Buddha I was able to unattach myself from attachment, to unattach myself from self. It just went - POOF - and was gone. This is not to say that I would never again set goals or try to improve my station, or that I was discarding the idea of sin. It only meant that the days of obsessing over same, the days of being guided/judged by a theoretical construct of desire, disappointment, and fear were at an end. This had the wonderful by-product of thankfulness. If I set a goal and got all or some of it, I was thankful for and focused on what got done and not on what didn't. If I sinned, I asked for

---

measurable. As such it is maybe an nth degree of self-centeredness. It consists of nothing but full-time obsessing and involvement with mental theory.

[65] A line from Yoda to a young Anakin Skywalker, also from "Star Wars: The Phantom Menace."

forgiveness and was thankful for same. In both cases I simply moved on and went on with the day. In a word, how did I feel? "Free!" In another word? "Happy!"[66]

As a singer and musician, I know that musical notes can stand alone or be chorded with another. Certain notes go together naturally and make for good harmony. An A typically goes with a C, a C typically goes with a G, a G can go with a D, a D works well with an A, and so on. Each one is fine and true and complete on its own, but when chorded with a harmonious partner makes a fuller, richer sound.[67] This is how I find Christianity and Buddhism to be. Each one is fine and true and complete on its own, but when chorded with each other as harmonious partners make for fuller richer sounds: wonderful, beautiful harmonies. I continue to be a practicing Christian, but I find new

---

[66] As mentioned above, an alternate Christian translation of 'happy' that matches wonderfully with all this is 'blessed.'

[67] Oftentimes when playing with others, singing and/or instruments, I've had times when such resonant chords are struck that it causes people to do anything from smiling, to laughing, to getting cold chills, to even weeping. The purity and truth and beauty of it all strikes a chord with people's souls, I think. These type of real, observable, tangible experiences cannot be had via an abstract or even 'unaffected' self. Is the soul not affected by truth and beauty? Of course it is: it absolutely is. But also I think, by the *pain* of others. This is all Buddha was trying to say and is the heart of his teaching; that people can be and are affected, down to their soul, by *life*. And that the one unchanging thing *in* life *is* change, or *effects*.

insights and additional light and truth in Buddhism. I think there is such a thing as a 'Christian Buddhist.' I'm now one.

12 - A Jesus Prayer and a Buddha Prayer

In Luke 11 a disciple asked Jesus how to pray. In verses 1-4 Jesus responded with what has become known as 'the Model Prayer,' or 'the Lord's Prayer':

> "Our Father which art in heaven, Hallowed be thy name. Thy kingdom come. Thy will be done, on earth as it is in heaven. Give us this day our daily bread, and forgive us our debts, as we forgive our debtors. And lead us not into temptation; but deliver us from evil."[68][69][70]

The prayer starts with an honorific address to God. Working past the given personal pronoun, which most would agree is irrelevant and appears largely as a convenience and/or sign of the times and culture, the next two ideas are again on the lines of 'bringing God's kingdom down' to us here on Earth. The

---

[68] This is the well know King James Bible version.
[69] Some versions close with 'deliver us from the *evil one*.'
[70] The prayer's traditional close of "For Thine art the kingdom and the Power and the Glory forever and ever" is thought by many scholars to be a later add-on not spoken by Jesus in the original prayer. As such it is omitted in many modern-day versions.

way this is done is by us doing 'thy will here *on* Earth,' i.e. people living justly and fairly. The request 'give us this day our daily bread' is noteworthy in that it asks for no more than that: a sufficiency of daily bread or needs. It does not ask for surplus. It does not say 'give us this day our daily bread, and lots of extra, across the board!' 'Forgive us our debts/sins/wrongs,' is a request for mercy but with the understanding that we must do likewise. We must forgive, forget, and let go. 'Lead us not into temptation' is a prayer for help with all the above, perhaps the last most of all.

It's very easy to find in this prayer, spoken by Jesus himself, common ground with Buddhism. There is the idea of honoring God through our actions now, in this life, in the here-and-now, especially with respect to others. There is the idea of avoiding the temptations to form attachments: attachments that come by following a self-centered lifestyle, done in pursuit of control and in rejection of change.

In comparison here is a sample Buddhist prayer:
> "I will take refuge in the Buddha, Dharma, and Sangha
> Until I attain Enlightenment.
> By merit accumulations from practicing generosity and the other perfections.

May I attain Enlightenment, for the benefit of all sentient beings."[71][72]

It's very easy to find in this prayer common ground with Christianity. There is the idea of honoring a higher power, and that through practicing faithfulness, and much of that through good/loving/helpful relationships with one's neighbors. There is the idea of living a converted lifestyle now, via one's actions *now*, and for the benefit of others *now*.

There is a very real harmony between the two faiths. Christians and Buddhists ought to be able to pray *and* work together towards shared interests and goals, for the benefit of each other and the world-at-large.

---

[71] Buddha is thought to have said and taught this or a similar prayer.
[72] 'Dharma' and 'Sangha' are Buddhist terms for 'duty' and 'community.'

13 - Outtro

Writing this book has been a real labor of love for me. Examining the teachings of Jesus and Buddha in a side by side manner has been most illuminating. I hope it has been for you too. There are many similarities between the two great faiths of Christianity and Buddhism. As far as living in the day-to-day, both emphasize the ideas of being present in the present and not the past, of letting go of one's issues, and of letting go of the issues that come from letting go of the issues. Both emphasize ideas of peace, harmony, and balance: balance with self, others, and nature. Both very much emphasize the idea of rightful acting, and that what a person does matters, especially to others. Both would steer adherents away from obsessing over wealth and materialism and short-lived sensory pleasures. Both Jesus and Buddha would say that life consists of more than cramming in as much fun, entertainment, pleasure, and distractions as possible. In fact, both Jesus and Buddha would say that a self-driven lifestyle is a foolish and a wasteful one. Buddha might call this compulsive and dependent neediness, 'attachment.' Jesus might call it being a 'slave to sin.'

Both Jesus and Buddha would say that the happy life consists of self-denial and putting other first. Both would say this kind of lifestyle brings a certain kind of inner peace: a redemptive calm and restoration of the soul. Learning to live like this and successfully practicing it Jesus might call 'salvation.' Buddha might call this same kind of lifestyle 'enlightenment.' An alternate meaning of the Chinese word usually translated as 'enlightenment' has it as 'waking up.' Jesus might smile at that and say that such a lifestyle is "to be free, and free indeed." Buddha might agree with that, and also smile.

And yes, both taught that there is life beyond the grave and that while it consists of something outside of our knowledge, what we can know is that in that final, ultimate, place there is peace, bliss, and one-ness. There is no more suffering. There is no more change. It is forever.

I will close this study with a list of comparative quotes from both Jesus and Buddha.[73][74] Some are direct quotes; others are paraphrases that deliver the same essential thought. The answers follow.

---

[73] Jesus' sayings come from the Bible. Buddha's sayings come from his collection of writings called 'Sutras.' As Buddha lived to around age 80, there are *volumes* of his writings. The main body are called 'Mahayana Sutras.'
[74] For persons wishing a quick and easy and pop reference guide to some of Buddha's reported sayings, one such list can be found here: https://bestquoteslist.com/buddhist-quotes/.

Shalom, Ping 'An, Peace.

Thank You and God Bless

And

"May all beings be happy and free from suffering"

Sonny

Who Said It?

1) "Love your neighbor."

2) "Don't hurt your neighbor."

3) "Don't gossip about people."

4) "Quit lying."

5) "Don't commit murder."

6) "Don't kill without reason."

7) "Find a useful job, do it well, and be happy with that."

8) "Be content with your pay."

9) "Don't desire your neighbor's spouse."

10) "Quit having affairs."

11) "A little wine is ok; too much and you'll be drunk."

12) "Avoid excessive use of alcohol."

13) "Relax because nothing is in your control."

14) "Why worry? You can't even control the color of your hair."

15) "Guilty people shouldn't throw stones at others."

16) "Rightful views and intentions will prevent you from doing wrong."

17) "If you harm someone, make it up to them."

18) "If you have an issue with somebody go work it out."

19) "Watch the thought and its ways with care and let it spring from love born out of concern for all beings."

20) "With the measure you use it shall be measured back to you."

21) "Do not work and slave for things that perish."

22) "The trouble is, you think you have time."

23) "Seek to live in peace; avoid conflict."

24) "Seek to live in peace; extinguish karma."

25) "The truth will set you free."

26) "A liberated mind has the greatest bliss."

27) "Your worst enemy cannot harm you as much as your own unguarded thoughts."

28) "What comes out of the heart is what makes a person good or bad."

29) "Holding onto anger is like drinking poison and expecting the other person to die."

30) "And forgive us our trespasses as we forgive those who have trespassed against us."

31) "Everything that has a beginning has an ending, make your peace with that and all will be well."

32) "Blessed are the peacemakers."

33) "Don't get attached to things."

34) "Don't be a slave to money."

35) "Each morning we are born again. What we do today is what matters most."

36) "Ye must be born again."

Who Said It? (Answers)

1) J
2) B
3) J
4) B
5) J
6) B
7) B
8) J
9) J
10) B
11) J
12) B
13) B
14) J
15) J
16) B
17) B

18) J

19) B

20) J

21) J

22) B

23) J

24) B

25) J

26) B

27) B

28) J

29) B

30) J

31) B

32) J

33) B

34) J

35) B

36) J

BIBLE SOURCES

American King James Version - AKJV

American Standard Version - ASV

Berean Literal Bible – BSB

Blue Letter Bible - BLB

Darby Bible Translation - DBT

Douay-Rheims Bible - DRB

English Standard Version - ESV

God's Word Translation - GWT

Holman Christian Standard Bible - HCSB

International Standard Version - ISV

Jubilee Bible 2000 - JB2000

King James Bible - KJV

King James 2000 Bible - KJV2000

NET Bible - NET

New American Standard Bible - NASB

New Century Version – NCV

New International Version - NIV

New Living Translation - NLT

Webster's Bible Translation - WBT

World English Bible – WEB

Strong's New Testament - SNT

Weymouth New Testament – WNT

Young's Literal Translation - YLT

BUDDHISM SOURCES

"Biography of Buddha." May 2018. https://www.biographyonline.net/spiritual/buddha.html.

"Buddhism and the Skandas." June 2018. http://buddhism-guide.com/buddhism/skandhas.htm.

"Buddhist Ethics." January 2018. http://buddhanet.net/e-learning/budethics.htm.

Gray, Jason. "Buddhist Views of the Afterlife." April 2018. http://www.hinduwebsite.com/hinduism/concepts/creation.asp

"Buddhists and Funerals." September 2017. https://buddhisminter.wordpress.com/2007/09/14/buddhist-belief-in-funerals.

"Green Buddhism: Buddhism for Today." The Buddhist Centre, November 2016. Web.

Kimberly. "Three Marks of Existence." Buddhistsorg. December 2016.

Kornfield, Jack. "Identity and Selflessness in Buddhism." April 2018. https://tricycle.org/magazine/no-self-or-true-self/.

Lief, Judy. Daido, John. Thurman, Robert. "Fear and fearlessness: what Buddha taught." May 25, 2017 https://www.lionsroar.com/fear-and-fearlessness-what-the-buddhists-teach/.

Morrell, Peter. "The World as an Illusion: Philosophy and Buddhism." January 1997. http://www.homeoint.org/morrell/buddhism/illusion.htm.

O'Brien, Barbara. "The Four Noble Truths of Buddhism" Buddhism.about.com. Web. Jan. 2017.

Siderits, Mark. "Buddha." Stanford University.

THE BASIC TEACHING OF BUDDHA. San Francisco State University. Web. 2015.

"The Five Skandas." June 2017. https://www.thoughtco.com/the-skandhas-450192.

"The Four Noble Truths." The Four Noble Truths. bbc.co.uk web. 2016.

OTHER SOURCES

Arendt, Hannah. "What is Freedom?" https://philosophicalnotebooks.wordpress.com/2017/08/27/arendt-what-is-freedom/.

Aristotle. Categories and Topics. Metaphysics.

http://classics.mit.edu/Aristotle/categories.1.1.html

http://classics.mit.edu/Aristotle/metaphysics.html.

"Calvinism and Total Depravity."

http://www.biblelife.org/calvinism_depravity.htm.

Hobbs, Thomas. Leviathan. Leviathan. Broadview, 2011. Print.

Jayaram, V. "Creation in Hinduism."

http://www.hinduwebsite.com/hinduism/concepts/creation.asp Dec. 2017.

Jayaram, V. "The problem of Maya and Illusion."

http://hinduwebsite.com/beliefinmaya.asp. March 2018.

Kelsen, Hans. "Is and Ought in Kant's Philosophy."

http://www.oxfordscholarship.com/view/10.1093/acprof:oso/9780198252177.001.0001/acprof-9780198252177-chapter-18.

March 2012.

"The Historic Jesus." May 2018.

http://www.biblicaljesus.org/index.cfm/fuseaction/basics.tour/ID/2/Historical-Jesus.htm.

"The Real Jesus." December. 2014.

https://www.washingtonpost.com/posteverything/wp/2014/12/18/did-historical-jesus-exist-the-traditional-evidence-doesnt-hold-up/?utm_term=.a1f64628061c.

OTHER BOOKS BY SONNY SHANKS:

A CLOSET CATHOLIC COMES OUT—AND AVOIDS THE CAFETERIA

ANGELS IN THE BIBLE

HEAVEN IN THE BIBLE

HELL IN THE BIBLE

DEMONS IN THE BIBLE

DEMONS OVER MY SHOULDER

All are available now on Amazon as paperback or Kindle

(all titles all rights reserved)

Printed in Great Britain
by Amazon